says

Finally!

Moving Forward in Christ

God *says* Finally!

Moving Forward in Christ

Kimberly Armstrong

KASTRONG
MINISTRIES

GOD SAYS FINALLY!, Armstrong, Kimberly

1st ed.

KAstrong Ministries

KASTRONG
MINISTRIES

ISBN: 978-1-7340685-1-1

Acknowledgements:

I would like to take this time to thank God for gracing me with fresh Rhema every morning to give to His people. He gave me the strength, the motivation and endurance to complete this assignment.

A special thank you to my family who inspired me daily: my mother, Joyce Armstrong, my siblings: Ron, Chad and Ashley and my nephews Timothy and Emaj.

My spiritual mother/covering Apostle Dr. Shirley R. Brown, for keeping me focused on what really matters- ministry. I will forever be grateful for your prayers, support, time of pouring and labor of love.

My church family, MZCOD- The Healing Place, for allowing me to be your Senior Leader during this time of spiritual transitioning, expansion and growth.

Terri Wooten-Parker and Chandra Williams, I am so grateful for your assistance and dedication. You both contributed to helping me keep my material on track and well organized. Your faithfulness was very well noted.

~~~

The Dunn family (Farley, Diane & Steven) your faith in me and the creativity that you have been graced with has brought me to this place. Thank you for your support and your willingness to share your God-given gifts and resources.

~~~

I would like to thank all of those who were inspired by the daily quotes that I released on social media. It was your push for more that encouraged me to post something new and fresh every morning. Your personal testimonies motivated me to continue to inspire others.

A Note from Kimberly Armstrong

My first book, *Morning Jarva*, was the lead into *Finally*. It was during this season that I could not see my way out of what God was doing in my life. There were times in which I asked myself, will this wilderness experience ever come to an end? He quickly made me aware that what He was doing was greater than what I could ever imagine. This was my time for processing and preparation.

All I had was my Faith in Jesus. I knew that He was with me and would never leave me. He was my strength and my praise during the times I was challenged with all types of attacks, hurts and disappointments. Nevertheless, my Anchor, Jesus, never gave me any reason to give up!

As you advance in the Kingdom of God, many paths will be presented to you. However, make sure the one you choose is the one God has ordained. He will see you through all of your uncertainties. He will be your light in the midst of darkness. He will be the peace that calms all your fears. He will lead and guide you up the hill, through the valley and around the mountain. He brings you to that place called "There." If you can hold on and fight the good fight of faith, you too will meet Finally!

When you meet Finally, He's not going to look like what you had envisioned. Your fleshly finally and your Godly Finally are none of the same. You see, your flesh will be anxious and have all kinds of expectations. Sort of like fish that have just been caught by a fisherman. When the fisherman takes the fish off his line, he places it inside of a cooler. While there, the fish begins to jump and make thumping noises as if to say, I will get out and return to my natural habitation. However, as time begins to pass, the fisherman goes and checks on the fish. They are not as active as they were initially. He shuts the lid to the cooler. He later goes back to check and they are barely moving. He does this until there are no signs of life or struggle. It is at that time, the fisherman says, "Okay, now I can clean you and prepare you for what I need."

So it is with God. At the time God moves in your life, you will know that it's truly Him.

How, you may ask? He will allow you to go through a process that will cause you to lose all desires to please self. It will not feel like you had hoped it would. No bells and whistles. It will not be celebratory nor will there be much excitement. It will be a "nevertheless not my will but thy will be done" kind of moment. This is when the flesh is no longer in control but has yielded to the Spirit. It is in this moment that God says, Finally you can move forward in Christ! You are in it for My glory and not for any other reason. Enjoy your journey. Finally is finally here.

Accept who you are and walk in your calling.

_____

_____

_____

_____

_____

_____

_____

_____

_____

_____

_____

_____

You can move in confidence, knowing that what God began so shall He complete!

_____

_____

_____

_____

_____

_____

_____

_____

_____

_____

_____

You can be at peace, knowing that God is your Heavenly Father tending to earthly matters!

_____

_____

_____

_____

_____

_____

_____

_____

_____

_____

_____

_____

_____

_____

You have learned how to rely on Jesus for those things that are beyond your control!

_____

_____

_____

_____

_____

_____

_____

_____

_____

_____

_____

_____

_____

By Faith, you are able to accept that all things are truly working together for your Good!

_____

_____

_____

_____

_____

_____

_____

_____

_____

_____

_____

_____

_____

You realize God will deliver again, because He did so way back then!

_____

_____

_____

_____

_____

_____

_____

_____

_____

_____

_____

_____

You can see what God said would be! Praise Him!

_____

_____

_____

_____

_____

_____

_____

_____

_____

_____

_____

_____

Finally!
says
Moving Forward in Christ

You have come to appreciate God's Agape love! He loves you for you!

_____

_____

_____

_____

_____

_____

_____

_____

_____

_____

_____

Be thankful and just know that God will take the bitter and make it sweet!

_____

_____

_____

_____

_____

_____

_____

_____

_____

_____

_____

says

Finally!
Moving Forward in Christ

You understand the Power in Praise! Praise your way out!

_____

_____

_____

_____

_____

_____

_____

_____

_____

_____

_____

_____

_____

You must become happy being you!

_____

_____

_____

_____

_____

_____

_____

_____

_____

_____

_____

_____

No matter what, giving up must not be a part of your spiritual lineage!

_____

_____

_____

_____

_____

_____

_____

_____

_____

_____

_____

_____

Do not let the weaknesses of others deter you from your assignment!

_____

_____

_____

_____

_____

_____

_____

_____

_____

_____

_____

_____

_____

says

Finally!

Moving Forward in Christ

Find your rest in the labor and works of Jesus!

_____

_____

_____

_____

_____

_____

_____

_____

_____

_____

_____

_____

says

Finally!

Moving Forward in Christ

Make doing what's right a Lifestyle and not a moment-by-moment decision!!!

_____

_____

_____

_____

_____

_____

_____

_____

_____

_____

_____

_____

_____

says Finally!
Moving Forward in Christ

You realize that no matter how cloudy the day may get, it's not enough to make you walk away from the Son!

_____

_____

_____

_____

_____

_____

_____

_____

_____

_____

_____

_____

_____

You have learned that your life matters and the Kingdom of God is in need of you!

_____

_____

_____

_____

_____

_____

_____

_____

_____

_____

_____

_____

_____

_____

Originality is always welcomed!

_____

_____

_____

_____

_____

_____

_____

_____

_____

_____

_____

_____

_____

_____

Know the importance of Trying Again!

_____

_____

_____

_____

_____

_____

_____

_____

_____

_____

_____

_____

_____

says
Finally!
Moving Forward in Christ

Encourage others as you encourage yourself!

_____

_____

_____

_____

_____

_____

_____

_____

_____

_____

_____

_____

_____

_____

Jesus understands!

_____

_____

_____

_____

_____

_____

_____

_____

_____

_____

_____

_____

_____

Don't get caught up in the false returns of others!

_____

_____

_____

_____

_____

_____

_____

_____

_____

_____

_____

_____

Prayer is the key to solving life's challenges!

_____

_____

_____

_____

_____

_____

_____

_____

_____

_____

_____

_____

_____

Wait on the Lord; He will renew your strength!

_____

_____

_____

_____

_____

_____

_____

_____

_____

_____

_____

_____

_____

_____

says

Finally!

Moving Forward in Christ

Remember, God has charged Angels Over You!

_____

_____

_____

_____

_____

_____

_____

_____

_____

_____

_____

says
Finally!
Moving Forward in Christ

Always take God's Word over man's word any day!

_____

_____

_____

_____

_____

_____

_____

_____

_____

_____

_____

Jesus is the secret combination to unlocking your level of success!!

_____

_____

_____

_____

_____

_____

_____

_____

_____

_____

_____

_____

_____

_____

Stay the course!

_____

_____

_____

_____

_____

_____

_____

_____

_____

_____

_____

_____

_____

_____

Hold on to your peace!

_____

_____

_____

_____

_____

_____

_____

_____

_____

_____

_____

_____

_____

God is amazing and excellent in all of His Ways!

_____

_____

_____

_____

_____

_____

_____

_____

_____

_____

_____

_____

_____

says

Finally!

Moving Forward in Christ

Moving forward is a promise not just an option!

_____

_____

_____

_____

_____

_____

_____

_____

_____

_____

_____

_____

Pray, Wait, and Listen, then Respond!!

_____

_____

_____

_____

_____

_____

_____

_____

_____

_____

_____

_____

Wake up to truth and let go of the should've, could've and would've!

_____

_____

_____

_____

_____

_____

_____

_____

_____

_____

_____

_____

_____

Recognize that growth comes with newfound Revelations … Not rehearsed patterns!

_____

_____

_____

_____

_____

_____

_____

_____

_____

_____

_____

_____

_____

_____

Finally!
Moving Forward in Christ

Be thankful for spiritual coverage with surveillance and/or onsite technicians!

_____

_____

_____

_____

_____

_____

_____

_____

_____

_____

_____

_____

_____

Celebrate You … Don't wait for Others to!

_____

_____

_____

_____

_____

_____

_____

_____

_____

_____

_____

_____

_____

_____

Remember it is you that God loves, not your possessions!

_____

_____

_____

_____

_____

_____

_____

_____

_____

_____

_____

_____

_____

God's timing works best ... He never arrives late!

_____

_____

_____

_____

_____

_____

_____

_____

_____

_____

_____

_____

Never underestimate the power of Love! It kept Jesus on the Cross until the work was finished!

_____

_____

_____

_____

_____

_____

_____

_____

_____

_____

_____

_____

_____

Finally!

says

Moving Forward in Christ

It's good to know that Jesus will always be Your Forever!

_____

_____

_____

_____

_____

_____

_____

_____

_____

_____

_____

_____

_____

Finally! says
Moving Forward in Christ

If you have Jesus, defeat will never be your Portion. You will always rise!

_____

_____

_____

_____

_____

_____

_____

_____

_____

_____

_____

_____

_____

Your process is your Testimony!

_____

_____

_____

_____

_____

_____

_____

_____

_____

_____

_____

_____

_____

Rest in knowing that your ending will be Greater than your beginning!

_____

_____

_____

_____

_____

_____

_____

_____

_____

_____

_____

_____

_____

What is important to you may not be to others.
However, this is your assignment and not theirs.
Remember that Jesus is your Advocator!

_____

_____

_____

_____

_____

_____

_____

_____

_____

_____

_____

_____

Moving while yet standing still will give you an up-close and personal view of your enemy's Defeat!

_____

_____

_____

_____

_____

_____

_____

_____

_____

_____

_____

_____

says
Finally!
Moving Forward in Christ

Time has a way of bringing all good things to you!

_____

_____

_____

_____

_____

_____

_____

_____

_____

_____

_____

_____

God says Finally!   **91**

God will fight for you as long as you trust that He will win!

_____

_____

_____

_____

_____

_____

_____

_____

_____

_____

_____

_____

Finally!
Moving Forward in Christ

Feel the freedom to move out into the new. He called you forth to display what true relationship in Him really looks like!

_____

_____

_____

_____

_____

_____

_____

_____

_____

_____

_____

_____

There is no one that will love you like Jesus. In your natural setting He sees your good, your bad and your ugly. But He loves you for you!

_____

_____

_____

_____

_____

_____

_____

_____

_____

_____

_____

_____

Be mindful of how you treat your Spiritual Coverings. It is a true sign of how you treat God!

_____

_____

_____

_____

_____

_____

_____

_____

_____

_____

_____

_____

_____

_____

Find someone that will pour into you without having a problem with where God is taking you!

_____

_____

_____

_____

_____

_____

_____

_____

_____

_____

_____

_____

When you pray, Expect Results. Heaven is waiting to Respond!

_____

_____

_____

_____

_____

_____

_____

_____

_____

_____

_____

_____

_____

Never give up on you. Why? Because it is you that God will use to advance His kingdom and not religion!!

_____

_____

_____

_____

_____

_____

_____

_____

_____

_____

_____

_____

Remember man gives you the right to remain silent but God gives a command that we must Praise Him regardless!!!

_____

_____

_____

_____

_____

_____

_____

_____

_____

_____

_____

_____

For the Believers, change is a cue that something great is forthcoming. Welcome it and walk it out!!

Be responsible for your own actions. Only you can choose to maximize your potential in order to get maximum results!

_____

_____

_____

_____

_____

_____

_____

_____

_____

_____

_____

_____

_____

_____

You are stronger than you think! God took your weakness and made you Strong!!

_____

_____

_____

_____

_____

_____

_____

_____

_____

_____

_____

_____

_____

You were built for this! Stop doubting yourself and stand in the Power of God!!

_____

_____

_____

_____

_____

_____

_____

_____

_____

_____

_____

_____

If you are a leader, it is important that you lead right, be right and stay right!! Someone's spiritual life is at stake.

_____

_____

_____

_____

_____

_____

_____

_____

_____

_____

_____

_____

Pay close attention to new patterns in your life.
They are leading you somewhere. Stay alert!!

_____

_____

_____

_____

_____

_____

_____

_____

_____

_____

_____

_____

_____

_____

*Let time be your friend. Start to enjoy the moment
instead of rushing through or wasting it!*

_____

_____

_____

_____

_____

_____

_____

_____

_____

_____

_____

_____

_____

Can you fill this position today ... the job title is:
Worshipper?

_____

_____

_____

_____

_____

_____

_____

_____

_____

_____

_____

_____

_____

Never underestimate your worth. If you do, you'll never operate at the level for which you were built!

_____

_____

_____

_____

_____

_____

_____

_____

_____

_____

_____

Knowing who you are does not make you arrogant,
but confident and for the believers... PECULIAR!

_____

_____

_____

_____

_____

_____

_____

_____

_____

_____

_____

_____

Sometimes having someone to listen without passing judgment is all it takes for recovery!!

_____

_____

_____

_____

_____

_____

_____

_____

_____

_____

_____

_____

Don't despise Change. It is a good indicator that God can trust you at and on that level!

_____

_____

_____

_____

_____

_____

_____

_____

_____

_____

_____

_____

God says Finally!
Moving Forward in Christ

God is waiting on you to take control of your emotions and realize that only you can do this... not your neighbor!!!

_____

_____

_____

_____

_____

_____

_____

_____

_____

_____

_____

_____

_____

God knows your address, your thoughts and well wishes. He knew them before you did and He also has them ready for an appointed season and time!

_____

_____

_____

_____

_____

_____

_____

_____

_____

_____

_____

_____

_____

*Saying good-bye to the old and welcoming the new
is granting God access to bless your ground!!*

_____

_____

_____

_____

_____

_____

_____

_____

_____

_____

_____

_____

says
Finally!
Moving Forward in Christ

Start looking to see God in everything and in everyone ... then you will find the Goods!

_____

_____

_____

_____

_____

_____

_____

_____

_____

_____

_____

_____

_____

Do not be so swayed by the way others feel about God's delays that you miss His punctuality in your own Life!!

_____

_____

_____

_____

_____

_____

_____

_____

_____

_____

_____

_____

_____

_____

*You are loved by a God that produces thoughts
and Births out Dreams!!*

_____

_____

_____

_____

_____

_____

_____

_____

_____

_____

_____

_____

Take note of where you are right now and know that it was God's Grace that brought you. That's why you are well equipped and above able!!

_____

_____

_____

_____

_____

_____

_____

_____

_____

_____

_____

_____

When you have an ear to hear and you follow instructions that can only come from God ... you will always be successful!!

_____

_____

_____

_____

_____

_____

_____

_____

_____

_____

_____

_____

_____

In your time of unrest, God will hide, keep and preserve you ... Trust Him in that place!!

_____

_____

_____

_____

_____

_____

_____

_____

_____

_____

_____

_____

_____

says
Finally!
Moving Forward in Christ

No one ever loses if they confess Jesus as their personal Savior. He always rises!!

_____

_____

_____

_____

_____

_____

_____

_____

_____

_____

_____

_____

_____

You can see what God said would be … it's here now!!

_____

_____

_____

_____

_____

_____

_____

_____

_____

_____

_____

_____

_____

_____

_____

Things are good now, but your good is going to turn into your Overflow!!

_____

_____

_____

_____

_____

_____

_____

_____

_____

_____

_____

_____

_____

_____

says
Finally!
Moving Forward in Christ

The enemy retreated because the onslaught on you was just aborted by God our Heavenly Father!!

_____

_____

_____

_____

_____

_____

_____

_____

_____

_____

_____

_____

_____

Finally!
says
Moving Forward in Christ

What you say will determine what God will or will not do!

_____

_____

_____

_____

_____

_____

_____

_____

_____

_____

_____

_____

_____

_____

says
Finally!
Moving Forward in Christ

We must adhere to the Word of God and not be influenced by the words of man!

_____

_____

_____

_____

_____

_____

_____

_____

_____

_____

_____

_____

_____

God has you where He needs you to be. You are on schedule despite your current situation!!

_____

_____

_____

_____

_____

_____

_____

_____

_____

_____

_____

_____

_____

says
Finally!

Moving Forward in Christ

The steps that you are taking are in sync with the ones God ordered!!

_____

_____

_____

_____

_____

_____

_____

_____

_____

_____

_____

_____

_____

says
Finally!
Moving Forward in Christ

If you won't believe Me (says God), then why do you believe them?

_____

_____

_____

_____

_____

_____

_____

_____

_____

_____

_____

_____

_____

About Kimberly Armstrong . . .

Apostle Kimberly Armstrong, is the daughter of Mrs. Joyce Armstrong and the late Mr. William H. Armstrong of Mount Olive, North Carolina. She currently resides in Goldsboro, North Carolina. Apostle Armstrong is a powerful woman of God who with grace, commitment, and passion serves as Senior Pastor of Mount Zion Church of Deliverance- The Healing Place in Calypso, North Carolina. She is also the Founder of KASTRONG Ministries, Goldsboro, North Carolina, a ministry of empowerment that is designed to reach the broken in spirit. She has been called for "such a time as this" to bring a message of deliverance to the shackled in spirit and healing to the broken with a cutting-edge delivery that changes all who come into her presence.

The Word she brings forth is founded in the bedrock of Scripture and ignited by the Holy Spirit to enrich, challenge and inspire the hearts and souls of God's people. Apostle Armstrong ministers the unadulterated Word of God with such a revelatory yet practical teaching gift, it reaches all hearers directly at their point of need and ushers them into a place of eternal freedom. She ministers with authority and clarity. Her objective is to deliver the uncompromising Word of God so that people will be propelled into living the Word and applying it to their everyday walk. She will encourage, equip and empower every hearer with the written and spoken Word. Her warm heart and giving spirit are immeasurable.

For many years, she has worked diligently with the youth throughout the state of North Carolina. She has held many professional positions ranging from President of Majestic Shalom Ministries Inc.; Founder and Executive Director of The Connect Four Family Program, Goldsboro, North Carolina; Director of the Upward Bound Program at Fayetteville State University; to that of working as an Administrator within the Wayne County Public School System. Her educational background ranges from an Associate Degree in Developmental Disabilities, a Bachelor's Degree in Psychology, to that of a Master's Degree in Administration. She wants you to know that the most important aspect in her life is her relationship with God and being an ambassador for the Kingdom of God. She is tearing down satanic strongholds and helping others get their breakthrough in God. This is worth more than words can ever express. God is doing great things through this consecrated vessel.